You Can Love You

Allanah Bahnsen
www.balancedbeing.com.au

Front Cover Photo by Simone Moore

Any reproduction, republication or other distribution of this work including without limitation, the duplication, scanning, uploading and making available via the internet or any other means without the express permission of the publisher is illegal and punishable by law and the knowing acquisition of an unauthorised reproduction may subject acquirer to liability. Please purchase on authorised electronic or print editions of this work and do not participate in or encourage electronic piracy of copyrighted materials. Your support of the author is appreciated.

Copyright © 2011 Allanah Bahnsen
All rights reserved.
ISBN 978-0-9871703-0-9

TABLE OF CONTENTS

1	To You	1
2	Beliefs as my Truth	8
3	Self Love	11
4	Selfishness vs. Self Love	15
5	Loving You	18
6	Low Self Esteem	20
7	Self Assessment	23
8	Wellbeing	27
9	Detoxing	31
10	The Mask of Love	34
11	Playing the Victim	37
12	Your Purpose	41
13	Chaos is Perfect Order	44
14	Choices	46
15	Transformation	48
16	Mind vs. Heart	51
17	Creation	54
18	Love & Joy as a Priority	56
19	Your Words = Your Expression	58
20	Self Love = Your Attention	62
21	Emotional Honesty	65
22	Moment by Moment Love	69
23	Forgiveness	73
24	Spirituality	76
25	Silence & Stillness	79
26	Anger	81
27	Compassion	83
28	Self Empowerment	85
29	Gentleness	88
30	Lessons of Love	90
31	Relationships	94
32	Working with a Mentor	97
33	Your Inner Child	99

34	Your Family Bond	102
35	Sensuality	105
36	Sensuality Meditation	106
37	Love is	109
38	Loving Processes	110
	Mindfulness	110
	Fear	112
	The Gift of Forgiveness	114
	New Dawn Meditation	116
	Heart Felt Clarity Meditation	117
	Heart Felt Clarity	119
	The Mirror	122
	Affirmations	124
	Decision Making	127
	Feel Your Heart	129
	Intentions	131
	Balancing Effect of Intentions	132
	Grounding	134
	Soften your Heart	136
	Emotional Freedom Technique	137
39	I Love Myself	138
40	Unending Potential	140

YOU CAN LOVE YOU

You can love you
But still not know you

You can love yourself
And be blurred in clarity

You can touch your boundaries
Only feeling your isolation

I love me
Therefore I am

I love you
Therefore we will be

John O'Sullivan
Bali
September 2011

GRACE

Be still
Feel your breath
The warmth you feel
is you..
it is grace
when you feel cold
turn within
feel your grace
release your pain
allow more warmth
recall you are loved...
believe
surrender
to grace...

Allanah Bahnsen
Feb 2009

1
TO YOU

This book is dedicated to you, you are loved! You can LOVE YOU! You are love. I am grateful to share with you, for without your heartfelt desire to learn about love you would not have found your way here.

Love is the only path to Divine Power. I am love. I am Divine Power. All my experiences gather here in these words. I have lived and breathed each of the processes and principles. It is my personal truth.

With open heart may you choose to feel what is right for you on your love journey.

It is exhilarating to feel what inner love is and even more exciting to know you can connect with it deeper as you grow. I have searched for unconditional love; love without conditions. My mother would tell me as a child, that I would not know real love. I presume she feared for me and believed

I had a 'pie in the sky' unrealistic view of love. Her unconscious projection was a reflection of the inner struggle of loving herself. I thank her dearly for lighting up my path, for it was in those dark moments of fear and confusion that I choose to know, feel and be love. Something was stirring.

I was born and bred into a cult religion that used fear to motivate. Fear of Armageddon, fear of God, fear of being exiled in punishment, fear of life and living it. I left at 18 and started another life. The mental, emotional, spiritual abuse layered my-self with fear and secrecy.

From a unique position, I observed the contrast of differing realities of life. I felt fear, yet had a knowing of my own love and strength. I had to nurture that seed and let it grow. I know what it takes to go from disempowerment to empowerment, it takes love.

My next stage of self love journey was to create my own family with husband and children, where I would feel loved and secure. In security I began to unravel my fears and emotional landscape. The journey back to me began.

I observed not enough love. On a journey to love, I experienced that which was unlike love, for the purpose of healing. My heart yearned for a deeper love connection that was consistent. That desire has charted my course of tuning back into source love.

Your journey will follow its own unique path, as you go deeper within, you will feel more love. A deeper love than you have experienced before. Loving yourself requires mind and heart shifts on a spiritual path. True love that creates worlds and change comes only from a heart space of compassion for self.

It is ironic how life provides the most perfect teachers and circumstances that lights up our unique spiritual path, perfectly in order.

Your unique spiritual path is to connect the tangible body of you to 'spirit' and to develop that connection deeper as you experience 'life'.

I started this book journey as a married woman when I received a vision to write about self love. I let my inner child come out to play. Waking up at 5am most mornings to start offloading the words onto paper. It was the only solution to get started. A few months later I went on my first overseas trip alone to Bali on retreat at the age of 37. On the last day in Ubud when I left the retreat, I left behind my birth name and changed it to Allanah. (*Al-la-nah* is the sound of my soul, if you could interpret the vibration of soul). I entered a phase of shedding skin, through a separation, divorce and began a new life. Re-birthed, I entered the world of separation. Releasing myself from karma and healing soul lifetimes loving myself all the way. It takes self love to release from the known into the unknown. If you are experiencing this path or similar, be true to you.

I live authentically and am empowered to create the life I want. My life is real and blessed with experiences of deeper love, daily that I relish.

Through the phases of life, I would also be delivered these potent words: "You do not love yourself enough". My heart literally hurt, it ached. I looked for concepts of what that meant. How did I not love myself? It was painful to learn I did not love myself. What was I yet to learn?

I was to learn that I had a limiting belief; I lacked self love and I learnt it may have originated from trying to win my daddy's approval. I had taken on my dad's pain of not being approved and accepted. He has done more than his share to prove himself worthy of the love of God, through devoting himself to his religion and beliefs and I worked hard to win his approval as well, yet I never felt his approval. This insight was only one level of accepting & understanding myself. I now had to take responsibility for my own needs and healing.

Simply put I needed to appreciate, thank and love myself. I needed to do this before anyone else could or would love me the way I desired. The self love journey is to understand all your emotions and reactions with compassionate love.

My desire is that you will find new ways of loving you as you use this book as a *heart space* to open your heart and live love.

I choose love moment by moment. There are no letters after my name and no recognised degrees in psychology. I do have the experience of my life, an open heart and mind. I follow my heart and embrace the continual management of the mind and ego. This is the self love journey. Life has handed me many teachers, mentors, gurus, religions, perceived limitations and heart breaking choices that have been perfectly timed to be here expressing to you. Your destiny is calling you...You can love YOU!

I acknowledge you the reader. You are a jewel ready to be uncovered.

You are LOVED!

My Mantra

The morning light speaks of new beginnings that open my heart. I offer this heart's yearning right now as I am, it is a divine pull of devotional surrender. I devote and surrender myself to love, fully. My heart's yearning is a hole through which divine love can be felt to emerge.

Love is who I am. Love is the gift I have been born to give. To live open is my practice through everyday life offering myself open in love deeper every day, loving self every moment as if the passionate force of a divine lover was entering me, opening my heart and body as wide as the universe shines. This is my daily surrender to love.

The Angels I want to thank:

My deepest heart appreciation to the co-creators in the spirit world.

Simone Moore my soul sister; your expression, spirit and heart art rocks my core, thank you for your creativity and faith.

The beautiful Rozi Clarke, Troy Williams, Julie Marsh, Michelle Campbell, Laurel Hughes, Michelle Long, Carly Warburton, Sharon King & Nerida Hunter for your authentic hearts and unwavering support.

©Allanah Bahnsen   All Rights Reserved   www.balancedbeing.com.au

Simon Toms, for your heart, compassion and love of dance and life.

Co-parent Matthew and all clients and friends who contribute to life.

John O'Sullivan, my light, friend and brother.

Marion & Ray, much love and heartfelt thanks for all that you are.

Beautiful Georgia, you were the catalyst of change, your mirror inspired these words...I love all that you are precious soul.

Earth Angel Cherie, you are my light and mirrored heart, your talent and wisdom are inspirational. You are love.

My beloved..

In love and light Allanah

These pages have been written from my unique perspective of the world, sharing my beliefs in a framework to the principles within You Can Love You.

You Can Love You is intended for you to interpret it in your unique perspective and position in this world. If we want to know your truth, you must create it because you are the source of your own truth. What is true for me and you becomes our unique truth and then part of the world's truth. In truth we are worthy of love, success and joy and it already exists in spirit, when we totally believe it ourselves it becomes our truth and it manifests in the material world.

The truth we seek is always in front of you but because you look for truth in places outside of you to be validated, you will never find it. When you stop looking for the truth it appears before you.

As a thank you to you for purchasing this book, go to www.balancedbeing.com.au/youcanloveyou.htm to download a complimentary audio entitled; I am or am I Love?

In honour and acknowledgement of Louise Hay the original self love queen and angel who inspires following section. Louise's work has been the platform for self love to emerge. Please read, listen, open and fill yourself to her body of work starting with, 'You Can Heal Yourself' by Hay House Publishers.

\

2
BELIEFS THAT ARE MY TRUTH

I am love. You are love. Love is my highest value.

I am a powerful being and creator.

I am an energetic being. Everything is energy. Thoughts, beliefs, illness and wellness are energy patterns.

What you need, you already have inside of you.

The more I love what you do, the more I will do what you love.

The present moment holds the power of creation. Be *present* and *listen* deeply.

I create my experience through the conscious and unconscious beliefs.

A belief is a practiced thought and therefore it can be changed through new practiced thought.

Compassion is felt within first.

Illness is created within by being at dis-ease or in conflict with ourselves, prior to the disease being diagnosed in the pathological stage. Every perceived illness within the body is created. Every illness, every symptom is energy and has a meaning. When the meaning is revealed and insight is acknowledged the energy of the illness or symptom can shift. Healing happens with acknowledgment and presence from a heart space.

There is no wrong and there is no right. It is how I perceive it.

I have access to my own inner resources through self love and acceptance. They reveal themselves in a self compassionate state.

All I need to love myself is *willingness*.

I choose to speak truthfully. I choose congruency of action with thought.

I choose to be heart centred and use the mind as a tool, wisely.

Emotional pain moves me to release the resistance.

My feminine/Yin essence is to receive and be.

My Masculine/Yang essence is to act, give, nurture and do.

Self love starts with action. Action then reveals motivation, then inspiration. Consistent inspired loving action leads to an organic shift of feeling love within. Self Love is a feeling that will grow deeper within you the more you act, think and feel into the following strategies. Self Love starts as a concept and then it deepens as your embody it.

©Allanah Bahnsen   All Rights Reserved   www.balancedbeing.com.au

Open this book to this page daily and find an insight for your day.

For deeper processes turn to page 110.

3
SELF LOVE
What does it mean to self love?

♥ Accepting you unconditionally, choosing to love yourself.

♥ To accept and love yourself, no matter what feelings, environment or what genetics you have been gifted.

♥ When you connect to your core self life force is there, always. You are love. Love is always there, if you seek it and choose it. Underneath the layers of conditioning, self loathing, fear, confusion or frustration, there is love. The layers have created a lack of connection to your heart.

♥ Self love is to choose love over fear. A cherished free choice.

- ♥ Self love feels good. It is nurturing, empowering and gentle.

- ♥ To gift yourself by changing your internal state from negative to positive. You give the gift of love and acceptance to yourself when you are grieving or feeling, by allowing feelings and healing.

- ♥ To have love for your spirit and it's ever fluxing vibrations.

- ♥ Applying love and gentleness to every word you utter, every thought and every action. When you are loving and kind to others, it is a reflection that you are love.

- ♥ Choose to see the meaning of perceived negative circumstances and transform it into love and compassion.

- ♥ Making commitments to you and following through.

- ♥ Self love means to be productive; Take care of things before they become a problem.

- ♥ Speak up. Say what you need to say. Speak with honesty and integrity

- ♥ Express your feelings without blame or manipulation.

- ♥ Assert yourself powerfully to enhance your own love and belief in self.

- ♥ Choose to challenge yourself, it is an excellent opportunity for more love and acceptance of self.

- ♥ Self development is the path of love.
- ♥ Creating and knowing your boundaries allows you to trust your feelings.
- ♥ The pursuit of emotional & mind mastery.
- ♥ Just *Being* is self love.
- ♥ Entering into a relationship with another is a lesson in love for self.
- ♥ Surrendering your defences as you trust your boundaries; is self love.
- ♥ Negotiating is self love.
- ♥ Give yourself permission to make mistakes.
- ♥ Assertiveness in making decisions is self love. It is self-valuing.
- ♥ Self love moments have a compounding effect.
- ♥ Emotional honesty and vulnerability with others is self love.
- ♥ Intimacy with self is love.
- ♥ Fearlessness within your own personal boundaries is self love.
- ♥ To allow others to see the real authentic you.
- ♥ To pause is love.

- ♥ To be silent is self love.
- ♥ Self love is a state of mind and state of heart.
- ♥ You can love you!

4
SELFISHNESS VS. SELF LOVE

To be selfish is to take more from another without consideration. To be selfish is to have no regard for another's feelings. It is an underdeveloped stage of spiritual, mental and emotional growth. Due to your fear of not wanting to be selfish, you get stuck here doing more for others to prove to yourself, you are worthy of love. Selfishness is a state of disconnection from self. When you are disconnected from your own love, you demand love from everyone else, do more to ask for it in return and will take from others what you can to fill yourself with the feeling of love.

If you are on the receiving end of a person who is selfish, it will feel like a sting. It will feel like someone has taken something from you without being considered or asked. You will feel like you had no choice, it was just taken.

This feeling, of having no choice, is also an undeveloped characteristic of disconnected self. It is a disempowered belief system. The premise of this belief is, "Others are more powerful in their wanting and taking I feel hurt and separated from them and my inner loving self".

Another belief is: "If I take what I want, there will not be enough for others." This belief keeps you externally focussed that there is more power outside of you then within. Learning to love yourself reclaims your wholeness and abundant nature.

Selfishness is based in fear that there is a limit of abundance and others will go without, when in reality your heart's desires and loving intent expands the universe and all that is yet to come into manifestation through your experience. This is the power you are yet to engage as a loving creator.

If old beliefs taught you to be selfless, you will be confronted as you relearn innate worthiness and value that is consistent.

You are here to create. What flows through you flows through others and into the world. What you become in the process of following your innate wisdom and desires with loving energy enables all to see your light and to feel your love. You share what you learn and discover through living love by example.

Dreams allow us to experience adventures and to allow possibilities. The ignition of personal power, passion, creativity, empowerment and love for self is contagious. Self love allows you to fill yourself with love, compassion and creativity that is expressed out into the world, unlimited and resourceful to all.

Love is within. Love does not require you to act or be a certain way. It is divine selfishness if you love yourself. By giving to yourself first and consistently your cup is full and will never run empty. The gift of life and love has been gracefully bestowed to you, live it with love.

There is no competition, only an ever expanding universe.

5
LOVING YOU

It is self love to prioritise what is best for you, after consideration of your feelings and then others. Self love allows you to make decisions based on love not from lack or fear.

Deeply loving all relationships in your life including you, results in love for all humanity, nature, environments and any form of life. Make decisions that prioritise what is best for you, it is the ultimate form of love. Your life, your experiences, your perceptions are unique to you.

Love others without requiring them to give back. To give more, you have to be more to yourself.

Go inward and feel every part of you, love your shadow parts, love the painful feelings. Take action while feeling your sabotaging emotions and loving yourself all at the same time.

Evolve on the inside and take more action on the outside, you will produce new results while cherishing yourself.

It is in changing on the inside first that affects the external. Healing yourself will heal your emotions and traumas and in turn heal your relationships with the world.

6
LOW SELF ESTEEM LOVE

Low self esteem love is the opposite of healthy self love.

A prefabricated, puffed up love is a cover up for low self-esteem. Feeling love based on being built up by others has no solid foundation as it is always prone to fluctuations from the outside. This type of love enhances the ego and the ego wants to remain in control by feeding on external power. It is fluctuating power.

There is a real stigma to not be a person who 'loves' themselves. This old belief system originates from being warned, not to be selfish and to put others needs ahead of your own otherwise you would be labelled as 'selfish'.

Ego-based loving yourself will be transparent. You will put others down to lift yourself. Low self esteem love is full of resentment, blame and traits of no-one is good enough – it yells of 'look at me' and 'I am better than you' and 'I want you to tell me I am good'.

What you feel around someone who exhibits ego-based love, does not feel good. You will feel their self loathing and your own will be triggered. You interpret your own self hate, denial and lack of congruency by being uncomfortable in your body and reacting negatively. It is in the reflection of another, that you feel yourself. You feel sensations strongly in yourself when others mirror you. You have learnt to label it, as "they love themselves" to avoid facing your own similar feelings of denied self.

Trust your amazing insight; you are wording the solution, they are loving themselves, the way they know how and are yet to love themselves deeper by feeling their way through their own pain and layers of self hate. They are on their way to self love. Low self esteem love is on the bottom rung of the ladder, metaphorically. The journey deeper into compassion and living love has began.

Understanding others opens your heart to compassion. Graciously receive the reflection of the mirror as more ways you can love you. In love acknowledge yourself and what you are yet to compassionately understand and love about yourself.

Healthy self love is strong, deep and goes hand in hand with humility. It is an inner strength that will not be destroyed with words or judgement. Self love is healthy for all those who are surrounded by it and feel it. It is highly regarded, respectful and inspirational. It feels like happiness and it is contagious. Healthy self love supports the body with energetic layers of warmth and gentleness around the heart, mind and body. You feel loved, in the presence of a person who self loves from their heart.

I demonstrate love through my actions.

Everything I do is without malice or judgement.

I show my love through my actions and through words of compassion.

7
THE SELF LOVE ASSESSMENT
– YOU CAN LOVE YOU

- ♥ Do I like the sound of my voice? Is my inner voice joyful and loving?
- ♥ Do I like to spend time with myself?
- ♥ Do I teach others to treat me with love by treating myself first how I want to be loved?
- ♥ Are you aware of your own behaviours and actions that are hurting you?
- ♥ Am I able to resolve conflicts without residual resentment?
- ♥ Is my sexuality expressed with love and respect?

- ♥ Am I honest about what I want to experience as love and can I share that with my partner?
- ♥ Do I authentically love myself around my partner?
- ♥ Do I give love away to others first before loving myself?
- ♥ Do visions of ideal relationships match with my reality?
- ♥ Am I inspired by my work?
- ♥ Do I follow my passions?
- ♥ Am I honest and accepting of my emotions?
- ♥ Do I take time to reflect daily on my inner purpose and am I on-purpose in actions, thoughts and feelings?
- ♥ Do I forgive myself?
- ♥ Do I forgive myself when I feel I am not enough?
- ♥ Do I forgive myself for those parts of me that I suppress or don't like?
- ♥ Am I accepting and loving the parts of myself that I yet don't like?
- ♥ Is my mental chatter supporting me as a loving human being?

- ♥ Can I sit with myself alone and love it?
- ♥ Can I sit with myself and reveal in the beauty and peace of the inner me?
- ♥ Are my daily actions congruent with my most inner thoughts, values and desires?
- ♥ Can I tell people the truth about me?
- ♥ Can I articulate my needs and values clearly?
- ♥ Do I celebrate just being me?
- ♥ Do I congratulate myself when I take action that is in line with my values even though I fear rejection and failure?
- ♥ Do I treat myself like my own best friend?
- ♥ Do I enjoy my own company?
- ♥ Do I expect others to love and accept a certain part of me or behaviour that I do not accept about myself?
- ♥ Do I allow time to sleep and value rejuvenating my body, mind and spirit?
- ♥ Am I allowing myself rest time during the day?

The answers to these questions give you insight to your level of self love. Opportunities to love you exist in each of these areas. What a wonderful journey ahead!

In Reflection:

Choose 3 of the above questions that you answered 'No'. This will be the best place to start and jot them down on paper.

For each of those 3 areas, now ask yourself these questions:

1. What do I need to do differently to reinforce a commitment to self love?

2. What would happen if I regularly took time to nurture myself in a self loving manner?

3. Can I schedule as priority, time and space for developing self loving actions?

Now ask yourself this question and write down the answers:

4. What actions can I take that will change the answer from 'no' to a 'yes'?

Now take action, diarise time, make calls and arrangements, release resistance and excuses and listen to your answers with love.

8
WELLBEING

Your body is a temple for love. Love your temple. Be with you.

Use your body wisely; stretch, meditate, exercise, laugh and breathe. Care for your body and for your energy. Your whole life is meditation of love if you allow it.

Being health conscious and having a healthy body is imperative to the self love journey. If you want to experience love, start with your body first. As it is your vessel of the experience of love. Love your body first.

Your body is a temple; treat it as sacred. Worship it! Love it. Receive pleasure into it. Treat yourself to massage and touch therapies. Shower it in pleasure. Bathe generously...it cleanses and reenergises you. Dress to enhance your temple. Adorn yourself with items of authentic expression that bring you JOY! Feel good about your body. Decide to love every inch of you inside and out. What you do not yet love about yourself and your body is an opportunity to love yourself deeper.

Nourish your temple with high energy pure foods. Bless the foods and liquids that enter your body. Your intent will create harmonious body functions, as a result your will feel supported from within. You are your own SUPPORT system.

Remember this affirmation; *'Everything I do for myself is enabling me to love myself more'.*

Getting good nutritional advice is so valuable. High energy foods + affirming thoughts and feelings= health & well being. Invest time and energy into finding and choosing authoritive experts and practitioners who can support you on your well being self love journey. Assess whether they are right for you? Are they practicing their own self love journey? Are they congruently on the path to well being themselves? Wisely assess your own needs and ask for help & guidance. It is your body, your health, you have the power. You can love you!

When you love and value yourself, self care, is a priority. It becomes a Discipline of Pleasure.

The old concept of, 'I do not have Time' is worn out, lose it! Change your focus to 'I do have Time' and watch time open up for you! Support yourself through affirming thoughts and actions that are aligned with your goals about your body and health.

Being obsessive and harshly strict about what you do is the opposite too loving, humble, gentle thoughts. Self care requires a mixture of self empowerment, compassion, truth and love. It requires being *kind* to yourself and being real about what is best for you.

Discover what feels good to you, like falling in love with another person, get to know yourself and what you like and what *turns you on*! Fall in love with you. You can love you!

Define what exercise gives you the most enjoyment and choose to see it as a fun, self love time. My body is more suited to low impact exercise. I choose yoga, daily stretching, dancing, walking, weight bearing exercise that keep bones and muscles toned, such as working out on a fit ball, joyfully swimming in the ocean after a run along the beach and more importantly than what I do, is what I focus on as affirming thoughts while I exercise.

- ♥ I am caring for myself, I benefit.
- ♥ Exercise releases energy I don't want, it is good to let that go.
- ♥ I love *being* in my body.
- ♥ I am capable of achieving anything.
- ♥ Increasing my heart rate...clears what is not love out of my heart. I allow space in my body and heart to re-energise.
- ♥ Being fit enables me to have more energy for what I love to do.
- ♥ Every cell in my body is loving and tender.

- ♥ I am listening to my body and its fears and lovingly embrace this as wisdom and lessons about me.
- ♥ I celebrate what I do achieve. I thank and appreciate myself.
- ♥ I Love ME.

There is healing power in taking short walk to clear your head and re-energize, no matter where you are. Just do it when you feel the urge, trust your feelings.

Invest time into your wellbeing and receive the blessings of abundant harvest of good health, boundless energy and enlivened spirit.

9
DETOXING & SELF CARE

Less is more; eat less to eat more.

Your body is a temple. How are you treating your temple? Have you cleaned your temple lately?

Detoxing is a valuable process that assists the body in ridding itself of unwanted toxins that build up. Every 'body' is different and processes stress, chemicals, food, environmental factors and genetic factors uniquely.

Detoxing allows the body to strip back layers of toxic build-up in organs such as liver, gallbladder, intestines and the skin. This loving process (which feels difficult in the beginning) creates clarity of thought, you will meditate easier and move more freely. Detoxifying allows for the excess acidity conditions to be transformed into alkaline friendly conditions. In an acidic body, you are deprived of oxygen and the acid acts likes poison.

PH means the "potential hydrogen" and the pH scale covers a range of 0-14 with 7 being neutral. All figures above 7 are alkaline while all figures below 7 are acidic.

Acidity levels of 5.5pH is a clear indication to a health practitioner that you operating from a state of mental and emotional denial. PH papers easily give you a reading. High acidity levels leads to inflammation of the body, excess fat, kidney stones, tooth decay and is the perfect environment for all the chronic 'itis' diagnoses such as sinusitis, arthritis, bronchitis etc

Value your body by getting the most up-to-date health advice from valuable professional experts and gather yourself a team of medical practitioners, herbalists, alternative therapists, holistic doctors, wherever your research and referrals from people you trust takes you. You are the leader of that team. Take the best supplements and pure food that supports your unique body.

Observe how your body responds and what results you achieve. The more nurturing you can be towards your body and the process of detoxing, the more the body will release gently for the highest good.

Do the most work when you are well. Do not wait for a crisis to self value. Be proactive and respectful of your body temple.

Love and value detoxification. When your nose is running, your smart body is trying to purge. Most in our society decide to take medicine, which basically says; "I want to keep this". The body has mucus, fluids, toxins and poisons and wants to be rid of them. Suppressing the natural flow will tell the body and the unconscious mind (which controls the body functions) that you want or need to hang on to the negative energy.

While detoxing biochemically you will detox negative emotions, it is a process of release.

As you embrace the detox as a loving process, your body intuitively learns to naturally detox again and will respond timely when the body needs to restore balance in the future.

10
THE MASK OF LOVE

The mask is social layers of conditioning. To be loved we learnt conditioned love. Love feeds us. If you cannot get it in its purest form then you will accept it in any way you can get it in order to exist.

Love is a basic survival need.

As a baby, you learnt early that to be accepted, to fit in with routines you behaved in a certain way. You moulded and yielded for the love you needed to survive. The disconnection began as an infant. You disconnected from source love, your hearts desires and from the truth of who you are. This disconnection created a program of unhappiness and shame to varying degrees depending on the family and adults ability to love unconditionally. Varying degrees of parental love is dependent on the shame they have internalised as they were growing up. If a parent was connected to their heart, then the result is a child who is more content and connected to their own heart.

When you are in an environment that is not heart based love, it is more difficult to stay in the flow of your own love. The signs of this sensation are subtle as your heart contracts and closes off. When your heart contracts your ego body takes over and feeds off the pain and you have disconnected from source love and the heart as the instrument that vibrates changes tune.

As an infant you recognised how painful this disconnection was and internalised it as suppression. You turned off feelings. This process shut down your heart over and over until you no longer recognised your true state of love. In survival mode you then focus on external love that requires you to bend, fold, twist and change who you truly are in order to feel love. The hearts desires are harder to hear and take on lower priority as your survival needs came up first. You can stop feeling your desires. This social conditioning can be explained as energetic layers of conditions over the heart, suppressing your own flow of love and heart energy.

It takes awareness and practice to understand the signs from your heart.

Naturally, children express their desires and pure enjoyment of being anything they want to be. Old social conditioning models require you to conform to please others and receive conditional love. Children and adults work well with boundaries and processes as it is part of the structure you & I need, to be fully integrated, managing our life. This structure will be formed with unconditional love or conditional love, with this knowledge it is now your choice to create a new model of your life that works for you.

Outside of the main caregivers you received additional signals from other adults who wanted you to behave a certain way to please them. You become a people pleaser, needing approval and worthiness. You changed the sounds you made, the words you used, the way you used them, all to be accepted.

So when it is time to ask yourself the question, 'What do I want?' It is any wonder that so many people have no ability to really feel what they want and desire from their heart?

Even the most unconditionally loving parent has a minefield of their own family and society conditioning. Awareness of this mask is important to define authentic love.

As you change from the inside everything changes on the outside. The shift's you allow contribute to the expansion of unconditional love and consciousness on the planet and beyond.

11
PLAYING THE VICTIM

- Do you feel victimised?
- Is your life a series of 'what about me' questions?
- Do you give and feel drained?
- Do you take guilt trips?
- Do you feel lost in your pain?
- Do you want to change but feel powerless?
- Do you ask why don't people see me or feel me?
- Are you feeling disempowered?

The victim role is not seen or heard in the awareness of a victim. It will be difficult to see until someone else, who will have been a victim themselves, points it out with heart loving direct manner.

The victim role is defined by feeling victimised by life, relationships, circumstances and events that you have experienced. It is feeling and thinking you don't have a choice.

As a victim you don't recognise when you give your power away. There is always a person or circumstance that becomes the centre of focus to 'fix' or to get justice from, so they themselves can be ok and accepted. Victims give their power away to others and identify with other victims. The identification with the role then manifests as a constant stream of experience of being taken advantage of, hurt and misunderstandings, of loss and could even be described as 'bad luck'. The role playing (ego identification) is not always conscious and is hidden from the analytical mind.

Victims seek negative forms of attention as sympathy or pity and look to others to validate their problems and story.

The role of victim has been assigned by you to you.

- ♥ Is anyone listening to your story?
- ♥ Do you focus on your story in your head or with others?
- ♥ Do you feel victimised? Sorry for yourself?
- ♥ Have you been unfairly treated by life, parents or people?

If you answer *yes* to any of these questions then you are assigning yourself the victim role. You are vibrating in your energy field – 'I am a victim, please help me' or, subconsciously 'I am a victim, pick on me, I am already hurt, used and sad'. Even though you may not see yourself as a classic victim could you be putting out into the vibrational universe a feeling of 'why me'? Does your emotional pain, want to be relived? Do you complain, become offended or outraged at the unfairness of life? If so, you are energetic victim.

Victims value others loving them first before they will love themselves. Relationships are a key area to look and discover if you are playing the victim role.

- ♥ Are you misunderstood and not heard in your relationship?
- ♥ Do your children walk all over you?
- ♥ Are you blaming your childhood for what is happening now in your life?
- ♥ Are you blaming your partner or children for your unhappy existence?
- ♥ Do you participate in family events not of your own free will but because you feel you have to?
- ♥ Do you feel used in your relationships?

If you answered *yes* to any of these questions, you are playing a victim role. We all do from time to time. Being a victim is a pattern and responds gently to change through self love. The mere observation of this pattern; begins to change your thought patterns.

Loving compassion takes away the victim's charge. It is a *rol*e. It is not who you really are. You are a beautiful, infinite, conscious being who can choose thoughts and choose new realities. Once a role is defined and with awareness, you can change your thoughts, feelings and actions to a new empowered state. With persistence and presence your external circumstances will respond differently to your new found self love and change into results that come from empowered vibrations of love for yourself. You must decide to stop being a victim and to recognise all the ways in which you are playing the role. Whenever you play the role you will be disconnecting with your heart's love and direction of purpose.

The only thing you want to control is your thoughts. Not as repression or denial but admitting to the existence of negative thoughts, understanding where they come from and why they have arrived and then with loving forgiveness and strength, dismiss them.

12
YOUR PURPOSE

"Your life is about the journey of learning to love yourself first and then to allow that love to be expressed fully in action, openly and authentically in every moment."
Allanah

You are love, you are source energy. Love is source. Source is the Grand Ordering Design (God). Allow this unconditional love flow into your being, accept it and extend it out to every other energetic encounter. Embrace the fullness of this love. Your heart yearns to take this journey. Open up your heart and let the love flow.

Your direction is the focus of your actions. Your purpose flows through every action and intention. Meanings and purpose are revealed to you, as deeper self love is cultivated.

Love is the reason you are here. God is love, the source of love. You are created in reflection of that source. Unconditional love is present and never changing. Your journey is to receive and emanate that love through your human body and experience as consciousness. The core of you is love.

The more you expand into love, the more there will be. Heaven on earth is the experience of love. Heaven comes from the Greek word Ouranos; meaning expansion. The more you expand into love, the more love is experienced. Jesus talked about heaven 'being within' and 'at hand'. Heaven is found within first through love.

You need love to survive and grow, to expand, to open up and to evolve, to broaden, to multiply, to swell, to stretch, to increase, to unfold, to communicate and warm ourselves. Love is needed to allow your purpose to emerge through you.

Fearful thoughts are: limiting, restrictive, resistive to growth, reducing love's capacity, shrinking and shortening. It will be fear or internal conflict that keeps out of your awareness the discovery of your soulful purpose. When your vibrational state is more relaxed and centred in love, you will be open to receiving insight about your purpose and the meaning of day to day experiences. Practicing emotional mastery by clearing hurt and resentment creates space in body and heart for this insight.

Your life is with purpose; an open heart and mind is the fertile soil required for insight to be revealed to you.

Process: Write a Love List

- ♥ What moves you?

- ♥ What brings you to tears?

- ♥ When you see or hear something beautiful that feels loving, add it to the list.

- ♥ Over time this list will clarify your love language, what inspires you and your purpose and will give you clues as to how to vibrate as love through action.

13
CHAOS IS PERFECT ORDER

Maximum Growth occurs at the border of order and chaos

Chaos works. It allows a breakdown before a breakthrough. Unawareness of how chaos works lets in fear, which overtakes actions, decisions and thinking patterns. Fear is the opposite to love. Accept that there is uncertainty.

Be aware of your fear and embrace the fear to let it go, allowing for a shift from chaos to evolvement. Be aware of the uncertainty and then turn this acceptance into increased creativity, alertness and more love.

It is through the tension of creating that you access a deeper love. In any one moment you can choose love or fear. In the tension of a moment, there is a sliding door opportunity of fear contracting your heart or love expanding your heart.

Consciously decide to welcome and smile at the chaos as a sign of growth and progress. Graciously honour this phase as more opportunity for love.

The resting place of the mind is in the heart, to find peace
within the mind, sit inside the silence of the heart.

14
CHOICES

If choices are made from fear, confusion and conflict are vibrating in your emotional body. You will attract experience of confusion and conflict. The conflict between what you desire and what you believe is possible. Conflict creates a neutral force of emotional turmoil and you feel stuck with no access to your natural resources within.

The ability to change how you feel is one skill in life that gives you emotional freedom and ability to experience happiness.

- ♥ Could you be gentle with yourself and your dreams?
- ♥ Could you love the resistance as a fuel for action?
- ♥ Can you surrender to the resistance?
- ♥ Could you love your health challenges?

♥ When you realise you have a choice to feel differently about your challenges, you are self love in action. You are an empowered creator of your own reality!

When you find yourself in an un-resourceful state make a choice to acknowledge it and remind yourself that 'this too will pass'. The softer and gentler you can be with yourself through even rough and harsh times, the faster you will move into an empowered state. The following self talk will disempower you.

- I shouldn't feel like this
- There must be something wrong with me
- I must be weak to feel this way

These thought processes lower your emotional state and create resistance. Judging yourself wrong for feeling bad, will then add guilt to the not so good feeling.

When you are angry or sad; really feel open to the emotion in a compassionate way. Let it be felt. Love the emotion. Own it.

The negative charge will release.

15
TRANSFORMATION

Your nature is your key to change; a negative can be turned into a positive. That is the spiritual path of transformation. The beauty in your character flaws are vortexes of energy into a spiritual journey.

You don't need to rid yourself of character flaws; you use them as learning curves to soul-filled life.

If you feel not loved; you start to self love; if you feel insecure your spiritual path is to look for ways to express through performing or humour so you receive the applause you so much crave.

The spiritual path is to grow using the seeds of character you have within. Your spiritual world and physical world are entwined and one, there is no separation.

Over time there is a slow reworking of the core character; negatives are turned into positives. It is in the challenge of change that you learn who you are; truthfully. People usually never perfect an addiction; the addiction will just reach a higher vibration. It is a constant reworking, moment by moment, that keeps you away from the lower vibration of giving in and acting out. The addiction is used by our soul to develop a spiritual path through challenge and self love. Through the desire to be fully in the moment and conscious of self you can turn a dysfunctional addiction into powerful action of moving forward.

Action gives momentum to the other parts of you that have not been so powerfully accessed due to the addiction being a driving force. When you access internal strengths that may have been suppressed and not given full expression, the addiction is no longer holding centre stage.

On this journey of change, other hearts around you begin to see your truth and reflected in their eyes is a glimmer of hope and amazement as they observe your courage in full expression of transformation.

The path of spirituality, never is completed, it is dynamic and every changing. You are energy. You can be a vessel of lower or higher vibrational energy; it is your choice what thoughts and emotions you dwell on (energy in motion). Energy is always in-motion and unending. So you are; always in-motion and timeless. The good news is that if you are vibrating at a lower frequency right now you have somewhere else to go, you can always just chose a better feeling or thought. Do you believe you are energy and everything around you is also energy? From this belief you can then jump to: A belief is just a thought I keep thinking, so if I change my thought then I can change my belief and I will change my life.

I choose to reach for the highest good feeling thought I can access right now and I will in the next moment make that choice again until I feel better. I know it is just a matter of choosing better thoughts moment by moment.

I choose loving thoughts.

16
MIND VS. HEART

To understand how your mind works is to understand yourself. To know your heart allows you to open to more love. When you understand how you work (what makes you tick) it is easier to lovingly guide your thoughts, intentions and heartfelt desires.

The mind is a structure that likes form. The mind finds it difficult at first to 'see' something new because it has no form or prior reference. The mind searches for memories, pictures that will somehow reference what you are 'seeing' for the first time. The mind gathers all the information, new neurons are laid down and the mind begins to form a structure within itself and you label it. (You give it a name) Forms are structures that the mind has focussed on long enough to recognise and memorise.

The mind likes to identify with 'things' that have form. The mind loves to identify with form. The ego identifies with form.

The mind loves ownership and believes 'things' make you happy. The ego thrives on being in control, superiority and a feeling of 'not enough yet'. The ego uses the mind as its structure to identify with things and form. The ego knows that no form is permanent. Therefore the ego and dependency on the mind alone, although confident and bullish on the exterior, is brimming with a sense of insecurity.

All forms that the mind creates are unstable.

Use the mind as a tool while learning to *feel* your body's responses and intuitive answers. Your mind does tend to lead you away from your heart.

Feelings of anxiety and insecurity are created as signposts to let you know that your *whole* self wants to be included and that your heart's desires matter.

Shadow personalities and sub personalities were created as you were developing as a child. They have helped you cope and gave you options at the time of not being resourced to access all your wisdom and power. Sub-personalities (which are created by the mind) are not wise under stress. The mind likes to take back control under stress and challenge and offers limited answers through limited beliefs that may not serve your highest good.

Alternatively your heart is wise and intuitive. *The Heart* is the energetic centre of the heart region. It is one of the seven major chakras. The heart I am referring to here is the symbolic heart. The symbolic heart and physical are closely related energetically.

The Heart is the seat of unconditional love, wisdom, compassion, forgiveness and strength. The Heart Chakra controls heart, lungs, liver, thymus gland and the circulatory systems.

Opening up your heart and accessing it will give you intuitive answers that matter. It will help bring balance to power/controlling cycles of the mind. Self love is to allow access to intuitive answers from the heart and to gently love and nurture the mind and how it operates.

Every religion, spiritual teacher and mystical reference refers to the heart in their discussions.

It is through the heart that you open up to grow and evolve as a human being. The heart understands your values, desires and purpose and knows how to direct you. Your heart has the ability to know your moral code, helping you make wise decisions that your sub-personalities cannot make wisely. (Due to their limited formation)

Your intuition is the inner voice of the heart that is loving, compassionate and real; it will always be true, even when the mind is at play. The more you access your heart and intuition, the more your mind learns to listen to the heart, the intuition and its wisdom. The struggle can end, harmony can emerge.

Feel Your Heart Meditation on page 129

17
CREATION

You are a creator and co-creator as all your thoughts, words, feelings and actions are co-contributing to creation. What you do today and how you do it is creating tomorrow.

When you love you, you love the world. You are reflecting love back to source. When you love others from a full state, you are, loving the world. Your heartfelt desires propel you forward to keep expanding the ever evolving planet.

When you follow your heart, you grow into your potential. As you expand, so does light, love and consciousness. You have so much potential to love. You can heal yourself and the world with your love. You make a difference. You make a difference by loving yourself first and letting your heart open.

Your thoughts and words matter to the whole. We are one. When you love yourself, you contribute to more love on the planet.

You are powerful, your breath is powerful. Your creativity is unlimited. Loving and believing in yourself gives access to unlimited loving power to create your life. You can love you!

Where attention goes, energy flows – James Redfield

18
LOVE & JOY AS A PRIORITY

Reconnect with your Joy! The Discipline of Pleasure; reconnects you with your love and joy. How you feel is more important than what you do. Every moment is an opportunity for experiencing the best feeling you can. You are not here to suffer. You have a choice to change your inner state in any one moment to something that feels better. Ahhh that feels good! You can love you and your life now in this moment by making love and joy a priority.

This may be a revelation for you and is transformational. What would it mean to you to put yourself first? How would that change your life? Make a choice and commitment to experiencing love and joy first!

Through spiritual practices such as mediation, prayer, yoga, psychic hygiene and soul communication, you experience the love of you. A seeker of a spiritual life is an explorer of love.

In touching grace and love there is the further invitation to experience it as a constant connection by embodying love moment by moment in any action or movement. Deciding to be joyful, happy and appreciative and openly loving does give a deep meaningful satisfaction to your life.

You can walk as if you are love. Speak as if you are love, as if a lover had just touched you and you have melted. How you open and close a door or reach for an item with your hand can be done in loving presence keeping you connected to source love.

It is your choice to consistently align with the flow. Attend to your own joy first and there will naturally be an overflow that will be felt by others.

19
YOUR WORDS = YOUR EXPRESSION

Your words are an expression of who you are. Your words give you insight into how you feel, what you are focussed on and what you value.

Pay close attention to your words; the words you say to yourself or about others matter. Words are self-fulfilling, your prophecy. There is power in your words and emotions. There is energy vibrating through the words you use to describe yourself. Your words are your law. If you joke in a self-deprecating way, are you painfully hiding behind the words and humour? Words tell. If you put yourself down or beat yourself up with words and thoughts, these words are expressing the parts of you that are yet to be loved.

Words can be swords and blades, cutting your connection to love. What words can you choose to speak with love and inspiration? Words can expand your energy into more love or contract it.

Every single word matters. Be selective of the words you say and label yourself with, yet not obsessive. Be aware and purposeful that the words you choose uplift and inspire.

Words create as they leave your mouth a sacred energy reflection of you. What are you creating with your words? Words are self expression. Write, speak, think, express with loving intention.

- ♥ If internal criticism is critical, kindly assess any truth to these words and rephrase for yourself what you know to be truth now and use these phrases to describe yourself
- ♥ When assessing yourself; use words that are compassionate and kind
- ♥ Judging yourself harshly contracts your love light and heart
- ♥ Find positive and enhancing words to say about yourself and others
- ♥ Use empowering language
- ♥ Choose words that feel good
- ♥ Use resourceful language that taps into your resources
    - I allow my inner wisdom to come forth
    - I have all I need within to take the next step
    - I can do it

- I am yet to learn how……
- All is revealed in perfect timing to me
- I choose to do this now
- I am *'insert verb or noun here'* now

♥ Reaffirm to yourself that you lead a productive and creative life and look for evidence of this in appreciation for all that you contribute to in the expansion of love

♥ Reaffirm to yourself that you a loved and you can share this with the world with loving choice words

Let your inner talk be gentle……

In your everyday life, shift your attention to a joyful and harmonious expression of life. Speak less of your problems and more of the good coming.

From a heart space, choose compassionate words in speaking and describing of others. Choose the most truthful words you can access that uplift and give another freedom to be, rather than project a limited perception through your words of fear, worry or low expectation. Heartfelt acknowledgement of another's inner beauty and potential releases them from limiting paradigms of being. Your intention matters and releases you and your attention to feel more love and joy for all souls and their unique journey.

20
SELF LOVE = YOUR ATTENTION

Where is your attention?

Are you in touch with your higher self? Do you have a connection and awareness of your soul and its desires? The depth of love for yourself will be matched by the people in your life. Choose how to love you. So where is your attention? Is your attention on your suffering and pain, on what you haven't yet achieved or is your attention on inspiration, gratitude and your ideas?

If you feel unlovable then your relationships will reflect and mirror you. The nearest and dearest to you will love parts of you and judge other parts, just like you.

Maybe your love is misaligned? Are you in love with the suffering and misery? Do you have your attention on your unworthiness? Are you so familiar with your story that your attention and love is unable to focus on moving forward? Are you so familiar with your comfort zone of love you have come to know, that loving yourself in deeper ways would trigger uncomfortable feelings? Uncomfortable feelings come from beliefs that we don't want to be someone 'who loves themselves' or is 'in love with themselves'.

Your attention to these old belief patterns will keep you afraid of letting the true you shine, as you are more concerned about what others think. It will be scary and unsettling as you confront the old patterns and beliefs. Remember, what others think about you, is none of your business. What you believe about yourself is your business. Let love be your highest value in relationships with self and others.

Is your attention on complaining and blaming? You can change that. Do you beat yourself up after making mistakes or for being not good enough yet? Where is your attention then? Is it on self love or self hatred and loathing? Like a magnet you will pull the same magnetic force towards you if you have your attention here. How does your object of attention serve you? What does it do for me? Turn it on its head by asking, what can I learn? What is the lesson here? What can I do next time? What will I do differently? Refocus on where you want to go and how you want to feel.

Take responsibility, take ownership! With ownership you are empowered, because you own it, you can change it.

If you have made a mistake, apologise and change your behaviour. Watch your energy change. Love yourself unconditionally right here. You are ok and you are worthy.

Be fully accountable but not at fault. Being accountable is different to being at blame and fault. With love and courage be accountable and responsible. Life is about results not blame. If you blame, excuses are available everywhere. This is a victim mentality. I know it well. When you hear yourself in this mode, pull your attention away from the blame. Remember: Attention = Love; whether healthy positive attention or negative suffering. Resolve today to change your victim status by taking personal responsibility for your actions, feelings and thoughts.

Defensiveness precludes spontaneity and creativity. Defending yourself is draining and contracts your ability to feel love. Why demand others love you by defending yourself? Love you first and let them find their own love vibration and watch how the dynamic changes. Put your attention on appreciating what you do love about them rather then what they are not yet appreciating in you. When they feel loved they will find more to appreciate in you. Attention = Love.

You can love you!

'All that we are is a result of what we have thought'
Buddha

21
EMOTIONAL HONESTY

Emotions are *energy in motion*. If you want to be highly magnetic, inspiring and moving forward in your life than you have to access the part of your mind which holds the emotional component. Incredible creators use the emotional component of their mind to thrust themselves forward into action.

Emotions are the transforming catalyst of darkness into light. Without emotion there is not enough energy to move forward from where you are to where you going. You cannot catch your future wave of destiny if you don't feel, your way there.

Do you want to access your own inner power? Than access your emotions. Access your heart's desires.

The biggest hurdle for a community, culture or singular person is suppression of emotions. Suppression is the act of not feeling and not releasing or sharing. It is also keeping quiet, blocking creativity and not letting self shine.

Anything suppressed (including energy) will be expressed (sometimes as explosive). The challenge in your life is to be real and true, to direct, release and trust the emotional energy in a creative and expressive way. If you are not courageous to express, feel, love your emotions you will block the energy flow. Are you in your flow?

Physical energy blocks appear in our bodies if emotions are not felt and expressed. The physical energy block becomes an imbalance in the body and then this leads to disharmony and dis-ease.

When the pain is felt, the muscle will tighten and cover literally the emotion. The muscle then decides as a conscious entity that it has a job is to protect the emotion from being felt by the body and the muscle becomes inflexible, stiff and hard. Emotional honesty is imperative for the flow of energy inside and outside of the body. The body is the ultimate marker of a spiritual life.

If you have a diagnosed disease the disharmony in the body has been in active disease stage for at least 5-7 years before it has become pathological. (A medical diagnosis)

Emotional honesty is to acknowledge your emotions and naming how you feel. Start with the simple things like taking time for you, not waiting until you are unwell.

Decide to speak your truth and be honest about how you feel, to yourself and caring loved ones around you. Be honest with those who can acknowledge you and let you express.

If you are asked, "How are you?" an empowered honest answer could come as this response: "I am having a challenging day today and dealing with it".

If you have a learnt behaviour not to be selfish; emotional honesty will confront you. It is just a habit to put others first and suppress your own needs. You were told that you would be acceptable and loved if you did this.

The old belief system has flaws that do not support your health. Therapy and honest communication with a skilled therapist can assist the now powerfully suppressed emotions to be released. Therapy and psychological reframing is a tool for mastering your emotions and thinking patterns.

Putting a smile on your face is an excellent way of changing your inner state from the pain/suffering focus. Receiving in love from another lifts and lights your heart. Self Love is the most enduring, unending way of rebalancing your emotions. Let yourself love you. Love all of your good and bad emotions. Accept them all. Do not judge yourself. Do not be in fear of your emotions. Your emotions are yours and they will never change if there isn't a loving and non-judgemental space for them to be felt and released. Just observe them and their meanings. Make it your intention to feel better every moment.

Bless your emotions they are the doors to your inner world and growth.

Love you emotions love your journey. It is your unique path of soulful expression.

Own your emotions, they are yours. Don't let your emotions own you...you have choice to release anything unwanted.

22
MOMENT BY MOMENT LOVE

Are there moments in your life filled with fear? Do you disconnect to love when you are focussed on tasks or goals that you haven't yet associated with love?

Do you stop loving and nurturing yourself in all the *have-to* moments? Where is your choice of attention?

How does that feel? Do your *have-to* moments feel harsh and pressured? Your power lies in the choice moment by moment of how closed off you are or how open you are to feeling fully open to love.

The more you resent what you are doing, the more tired and drained you will feel. It is never the task itself that determines how we feel, it is how we think and feel in any one moment.

Feeling small, restricted or limited is a moment of opportunity of choice to feel a better feeling until your circumstances change. Choose the next best feeling you can reach, it shifts your attention. If you feel small, it is ok at least to feel playful. It is possible to go from small and restricted to playful. It is not a huge leap in vibration. Playfulness is much more useful to expand than it is to sit tightly within your perceived limits.

The areas of your life that do not feel like love yet are opportunities for more love to be experienced.

The best way to move away from a job or business into *something you would love doing* is to love and appreciate your way there. Appreciate your way to the future, as if you were already doing, being, having what you love. Bring to this moment the feeling of how you would feel as if it has already happened.

Every moment can be about love. Find something to appreciate and focus on that. If you cannot find something to love within yourself and experience emotions of hate, irritability, anger and resistance then, then stop what you are doing. Reset your intention from the heart of why you do what you do. What is your purpose here? What are you passionate about? How can that passion be expressed here? How can you take steps to be doing more of what you love?

For example: Folding the washing is a perfect time to share love. Whatever the action, it is a moment by moment choice to allow love to flow through the action. Ask yourself; am I doing this with love? Can this everyday action be a vehicle for love to flow through me? How can I feel better now?

Observing your emotions, gives you insight into how you have reacted in the past and what expression was suppressed.

Disconnection to source love over time created pockets of fear that require present awareness to realign with love.

Love is fearless.

Love is the answer to everything. If you are out of balance, this is a lack of love.

Emotions are the guideposts as to how much love you are feeling. Observe your feelings to learn what you want. Observe your subtle preferences for 'what is love' and 'what is not love'. For a moment take a pen and paper and jot down without logic, in complete innocence; How does love look? What does love 'feel' like?

The more you allow your preference to be *of love* the more love will flow to you.   Choose love moment by moment. You actually have choice, once you know that there is a preference in your heart. The simple process of writing down, in a childlike way, without logic in the way; can reveal to you how you want to feel love.

Our highest preference is to gift back to source a reflection of love. The reflection of who we are.

Your ability to be of higher love and in your heart in any one moment means that you are gifting love out to others and helping them expand into a choice. You are helping humanity by loving yourself. 'I want love', is a pure desire, a choice over fear.

©Allanah Bahnsen   All Rights Reserved   www.balancedbeing.com.au

The happiness you feel is in direct proportion to the love that you give.

23
FORGIVENESS

To not forgive is too keep you away from love. Embracing forgiveness, embraces you.

Forgiveness is letting go and releasing you from an unloving state. Resentment, anger and hurt, hurts you more than the person you are directing emotions to.

It is easier to feel hurt, when someone has hurt or offended you, than to forgive. The state of hurt is the opposite of love. To feel your emotions is healthy and valuable to releasing them when the time is right.

Holding onto resentment and hurt is like drinking poison, expecting the other to die.

The longer you hold onto hurt and resentment, the more negative energy attracts negative experiences, so much so that you cannot enjoy the present moment.

Forgiveness is the commitment to you, to the process of loving change. The value in freely forgiving another is that you let go of the negative emotional state.

To forgive is a loving act first to self.

Forgiving yourself is one of the most powerful self loving actions that you can do.

In any circumstance, forgiveness starts with you, always. Even the most gut retching, evil, disempowering tragedy in life, can be a spiritual paradox of insight. Each and every perceived negative event gives you an opportunity to open up your heart into more compassion and understanding. You cannot completely forgive another without forgiving yourself first. Looking within to understand your own pain and hurt, allows you to compassionately find unique meaning. As you become aware of what you can forgive yourself for, then you open the door to waves of loving acceptance and compassion. This space of acceptance allows you to let go and release the entwinement of another being.

Daily forgiveness of yourself opens the door to gently loving and accepting all of you. Daily forgiveness empowers you to feel more love for yourself, as you forgive what you do not like or accept about yourself, you embrace all the parts of you and learn to self love deeply. Forgive yourself daily, for any unwanted thoughts, negative emotions that are hurtful. Forgive your shadow parts and their characteristic emotions. Forgive, thank and release others who may have played a role in teaching you a lesson about your life and purpose. End of day, is a perfect time to reflect if you have treated yourself unlovingly. Forgive and let go.

Process: Forgiveness from the Heart on page 114

24
SPIRITUALITY

Everything you do is spiritual. Everything can be of love if you let it be, if you allow spirit and love to flow through you. Even the darkest valley of life's journey and grief are opportunities for spiritual soulful expressions. All journeys are spiritual.

You are worthy and you are love no matter what you have done or not done in your life. You are worthy not because of what you do, but because you are! You are an infinite conscious being and can hold in your mind and consciousness anything you want to. You are not your thoughts or what you do. Identify your passions, your purpose and values and then spend time pursuing what matters. Set intentions and goals around your values and passions.

You are unique as is every other single soul. Everything you are now is perfection already. There is no need to fix anyone, just acceptance of who they are, will give you acceptance as well. With acceptance and compassion your inner world shifts and as a reflection your outer world shifts. Each and every other person in your life is on the spiritual journey with you, teaching you, living their purpose. We are housed in different bodies but there is an absolute energy connection that is unmistakable. Understanding our differences compassionately and the call to birth your soul and heart, is a great act of creativity to the world.

The visible presence of your body here is an invisible sign of divine presence on earth.

You have an ability to shine love and light into all areas of life mental, physical, emotional, career, business, financial health and relationships. Each area is an expression of your spirit.

Each of us is a culmination of soul journeys and richness of the intelligence and heart; inspiration and intention are powerful creative spiritual forces that are within you already. All that you need is within already. There are treasures of the soul that can be utilised by the logical mind and heart to harmonise your life here now.

Feeling spirit within you, being of spirit and allowing spirituality to move you is a basic human need. Survival is the most basic need, spirituality is a higher need.

One of the main benefits of spirituality is the exploration of the spirit, which helps you to understand the ego, personality traits and behaviours through which you uncover the authentic self. The ego self is not the true self. The ego is the platform to expand from. The ego's main concern is survival and balance. The primary purpose of the ego is to fulfil our survival and development needs. A strong unified ego structure is required first to allow expansion into a greater spiritual awareness.

Accepting & gently loving your ego (as if it were a child with a strong spirit) will help the ego settle and soften ready for your inner self to grow into more awareness.

25
SILENCE AND STILLNESS

Silence helps us feel through the aloneness to find our inner love. How we embrace this aloneness determines whether it is toxic to our system or nurturing. Nourishing ourselves in our aloneness is spirituality in manifestation. It is blissful and secure. A feeling of security flows through the nurturing in solitude.

When you are *present* with you and *aware* there is space to respond rather than react. Stillness and aloneness is filled with potential and contentment. Where there is loneliness there is vacant emptiness, without content.

When you know the joys of solitude, you will want more of it. You also want it for the ones you love. Silence and stillness allows you to be nourished from within.

Solitude gives you space and time to draw on untouched resources within. New power, insight and compassion are able to arise from your inner self. Reveal your better self as a result of your 'alone' experience.

Via deep stillness you can access profound love and satisfaction.

In silence there is an intimate union of all energy, God energy and yours. Meditation is the search of becoming intimate with you and Source. Whichever meditation technique or process you access aims at creating silence.

It is a personal preference which meditation technique you choose.

26
ANGER

Anger is a powerful emotion. At its lowest expression is hurts others and you. This type of anger is painfully raw, stifled and screaming to be released. When you hold onto anger, it hurts you. Lovingly release this anger as a positive expression. Go outside scream. Scream into the pillow. Roar. Sing loud, dance it out, paint, exercise and journal until the negative charge is released from you. Alternatively allow a practiced facilitator or conscious healer to help you release it from the body.

Anger expressed in its highest form through the heart is a form of love for oneself.

When you love somebody fully, your heart's wrath may naturally be evoked in response to their repeated refusal to offer their deepest gifts. Anger is then the deepest expression of love in a moment of being frustrated by another chosen limits and numb denial.

Through all emotions – your love yearns. Emotions are energy in motion, your loving choice is either allow that emotion to be empowering or disempowering.

27
COMPASSION

Transformation occurs when conscious awareness is no longer trapped in the patterns of the ego. Consciousness can take the place as an unconditional, loving presence that has no position (such as ego) and makes no judgement.

The essence of compassion is to be able to diffuse awareness from thinking something is bad or good through a process such as 'mindfulness', which readily identify patterns of low self esteem. With compassion for self or others you have the ability to observe what is playing out in your mind and at the same time being mindful through compassion to defuse it. Not to suppress it or act it out, just acceptance and love. Compassion feels like freedom.

Understanding oneself in compassion is transformation.

Self compassion is to accept without judgement or condition whatever positive or negative thoughts are going through the mind. It is an act of forgiveness and acceptance. It enables receptivity to understanding fears, perceived limits and or low vibration thoughts.

The more you observe the patterns of the ego in compassion and love, the more likely you will free yourself of them. The next time your feel critical, self blaming or self hatred, observe your inner voices, and get to know them without identifying with them or suppressing them. Just allow it to be and accept it. Extend compassion to the voice and emotions as if it is its own identity. Understand that there is no need to 'act out' or behave. As you hold awareness, choose to respond rather than react. The experience of suffering, self love and compassion happens simultaneously.

28
SELF EMPOWERMENT

Self Empowerment is expansive and it is self love. It is love.

The meaning of self empowerment:

Empower means to enable, allow, authorise, delegate license or permit.

Self means directed towards oneself, by oneself for or relating to oneself.

To empower yourself, you become the director of your life, emotions, reactions, feelings and your health.

Self empowerment gives you inner harmony, inner strength that appears on the outside as balance, grace, strength and as courage.

Empowerment in action is to see something disempowering or frightening and choosing to be empowered (self directed to act empowered) through the experience. Realising you have a choice is empowerment.

If you are in a disempowered situation, constant challenges will come until you learn empowerment and balance no matter what comes.

Every seemingly disempowering situation in your life is really an opportunity to empower yourself.

Empowerment starts with courage, then self love reveals itself, respect follows, when you relax, a space for compassion is created. Empowerment flows which allows you to stop butting your head against the challenge. The challenging situation can now be turned into something else and an opportunity for growth is yours.

Fear and confusion is disempowering. Decisions in fear create more disempowerment.

Compassion, love and gratitude are empowering.

As you make empowering decisions and actions in loving energy, your movement is complete, full and present. Complete in mind, body & spirit.

Take the time to align empowerment as a feeling before taking action and choosing the best path of action. This path is divine harmony in action.

Your actions are confirming universal energy that you are in fact in the right universe for the desired outcome that you wish to receive.

This is empowerment. You are a complete creator of your reality.

In gentleness or in intensity you can be harmoniously whole and empowered.

Imagine clarity and empowerment, moving into a challenge?

Imagine having access to empowerment and gentleness integrated together in your body all the time no matter what?

Feeling gentle and open hearted is self loving.

29
GENTLENESS

Gentleness is the opposite to the hammered feeling you feel once you sit still after much intense movement that is mind driven. When you sit still, does it feel like a freight train of energy coming at you?

This feeling is a result of taking action that was inharmonious to your whole and loving self and the energy hammering you has its own momentum built up from the disconnected action. It catches up with you when you are still.

To be gentle with yourself, is to move with presence and grace in a self loving manner. For example, walking, reaching for a door, sitting in a chair, reading and talking. The options for application are endless. Gentleness is self love, relaxing and calming. Be love within your body and move gently.

Allow Gentleness into your Body, feel the warmth of your heart glowing. The feeling of gentleness will allow you to talk to yourself and engage with others in a loving soft manner.

30
LESSONS OF LOVE

Have you been 'in love?' Have you had your heart broken? Has your heart been left with a deep sadness that love as your experience, is painful?

Lessons in love are real signposts to deeper self love. If you are experiencing pain, look within to find out why. The lesson in love is about you. The person you focus on is a mirror of your own disconnection and pain. When focussing on another from pain or fear, you are feeling your own pain, yet the focus is another person has caused you the pain. This feeling originates from 'Victim' thinking. What you ask from others is what you want to feel. Be willing to give it to yourself.

As a soul, you decided to come forth in a physical manifestation, to explore choice as a physical being. You came to explore love, all its facets and aspects. The opposite vibration of love is fear. To experience higher vibrations of love, you will experience the polarity -fear; of not being loved, fear and dread that you are not love.

Your soul and inner child are not happy being forgotten and rejected. The soul will stir up circumstances and events of disturbance to your love dynamics as lessons to 'find yourself' again. Your inner child will also want to resolve issues that were created with parental figures and will look to attract somebody to heal the issues through. If you could not resolve the issue as a child, the inner child will want to work NOW as the adult, to heal the issues. Lovingly your inner child and soul will stir circumstances of your relationships, until the lesson is learnt. Embrace inner child processes, through a professional therapist. Become aware of patterns to resolve the lesson.

The beginning of being 'in love' it is heady, powerful and all consuming you are entering a new phase of energy in harmony of yin and yang. The dynamic is truly a beautiful experience to live and breathe. It is beautiful also for onlookers to watch and connect in with their own heartfelt love, feeling love 'in the air'. Love will continue to grow and deepen if you stay connected to our own source of love.

The feeling of love is a powerful, chemical reaction over mind and body. It becomes dysfunctional when you are fearful of losing this most vital channel of love. Fear will disconnect you from your own source. The importance on another person feeding the love will have you twisting and turning behaviours from love-based to fear-based.

For example when love becomes so important not to lose it or have it withdrawn you adjust your behaviour and actions so that the love keeps coming. Even when it is not heart based love, you will need any love to survive. There is an unconscious agreement that you will play a role; 'I'll play who you want me to be and you play who I want you to be so that you make me feel safe and loved.' This is an expression of the ego.

Looking for love externally as your only source of love creates an unstable, unpredictable flow and form of love that you as the receiver will have to continually stretch, shape, bend and compromise for. Love is ready to flow out from your source to feed you emotionally, mentally, spiritually and physically.

So the experience of falling in love is truly a gift! It is the beginning of growth and learning about deeper love. It is yours to revel in. There is love all around, everywhere. There is intimacy (into-me-I-see) everywhere, tap into it. You can love you!

Experiencing love is beautiful, a soul desire that wants to be fulfilled. Love in relationships can be functional and dysfunctional. There are the vehicle for feeling love and happiness. Relationships are also the vehicle for experiencing that which is not love.

The responsibility for feeling love is up to you. No longer give responsibility away for the way you feel. Choose to love & accept everybody. The only reason, you are not yet loving everybody now is because you are using others as an excuse not to love yourself. Decide to love fully and open your heart. Be love.

I trust in the process of life

31
RELATIONSHIPS

Your relationships are a mirror of all the parts of your being. The mirror shows you beliefs about relationships and it reflects the measure of how worthy you feel. The mirror reflects all the parts you love and the parts that you are yet to love about yourself. Through your relationships and connections to friends and family, you learn about yourself.

Your primary care givers role was to reflect unconditional love to you and to build an emotional bond. This emotional bond is referred to as the interpersonal bridge. It is through the bridge that you learnt to trust and see the mirror. This foundational bridge was based on a trust that your parents where the very best of carers. You learnt about love through this bond. Your caregivers could only reflect to you a measure of self love, which they felt for themselves. The level of love they felt for themselves was developed through life experience and based on their own parental example. Therefore, every relationship you enter into is a reflection of the one you had with your parents. As this reflection was not perfect to all kinds of varying degrees, the interpersonal bridging developed in trust no matter what the outcome.

The way your parents reacted to you, will be the default mode of how you react until you choose moment by moment presence and awareness.

Unresolved grief requires healing with your primary caregivers. This grief work is facilitated through spiritual and personal development. Delayed grief is triggered by your relationships now. As you could not grieve fully or be supported emotionally to grieve as a child, you unconsciously create experiences through relationships now, to allow you to feel the unresolved grief. As an adult, you are in a safe environment to allow yourself to 'feel and heal'. These spiritual healing phases are self love in action. True love for yourself heals and affects growth in relationships.

Creating meaningful relationships with others is satisfying, if you are willing to enter into a satisfying relationship with yourself first.

Intimacy requires the ability to be vulnerable. (Into-me-I see) Understanding your boundaries allows you to be vulnerable. To be intimate requires you to risk exposing yourself to another, to bare your deepest feelings and desires. Opening up means you may be vulnerable to another judging you as unlovable. Yet if you hold the belief that you are love you create space in your heart, new space for equally loving relationships.

If you feel unlovable, it is a further opportunity for you to love yourself more.

Be assured that when your relationship with self is full, deep, rich and receiving, every other relationship in your life will reflect back to you a full deep and satisfying experience of love.

I graciously love all the relationships in my life, as they allow me to see and feel the real me, so I learn to love myself more.

When we accept all of ourselves, we are unified; all of our energies are centred as one.

32
WORKING WITH A MENTOR

"There are two kinds of teachers; those who take your power and those who give your power back to you."
Alan Cohen

Having a spiritual mentor means there is someone to take your hand, walk you through the layers of doubt and assist you to bringing forth your shining light of love and expression. A mentor with expanded awareness whose level of consciousness is more highly energised than our own will by silent transference impart non verbal, formless illumination of your energy and power. This gives us a subjective, practical experience of unrealised potential. It gives us somewhere to go. To become the vision that we are yet to real-ise.

A mentor will show by example that deeper states of love and higher states of awareness are possible and tangible when the student is willing and ready.

You may not be able to adequately articulate the exact reason why you want to engage a mentor or facilitator, yet there will be a surge of longing within to be heard, seen and understood. Self love and self development leads you on a path of willingness to be graced by an abiding faith that anything is possible and that you are only constrained by limiting beliefs no longer of service to you.

A mentor can see what you have not yet seen and can gently walk you through experiences and shifts to meet yourself in move loving and compassionate ways of being.

For further possibilities of working with Allanah as Mentor go to www.balancedbeing.com.au

33
YOUR INNER CHILD

Your inner child longs to be loved and have ongoing recognition. Your child loves to express itself through humour, playfulness, imagination and in innocence.

Love your inner child by listening and acknowledging the needs of your child. Self love is to love and give attention to your child, just as if a child was in front of you. As you treat yourself, you also treat your child. Space and time is dissolved.

A child is happy when they are heard, secure, wanted and loved. Just as children allow us as adults to see new perspective; your inner child contributes to a full experience of life and a deeper experience of loving you.

Asking a simple question of your child daily prompts you to connect what matters. By listening and responding to the child's wish harmonises the day.

It is up to you, how you let the expression happen? It is up to you to allow for the most authentic expression within your own daily routine and reality. A simple act with the mental acknowledgment that you are helping your child, is enough for your child to feel loved, today. Children are so in the moment they don't care what time it is, they are up for fun, laughs and play. If they played yesterday, they will want play again today. Daily giving your inner child expression, will feel nurturing and playful.

What matters to you and your child? Is it to play, dance, sing, skip, cuddle, dig, paint, draw or colour. Does your child want to go to the beach, ride a bike, make a mess, let go of responsibility for awhile? If your child is a girl, she may want to dress up and wear glittery shimmering items of beauty...she may have other wants. If your child is a boy, he may want to move, run, wrestle, play, ride, make noise, hug, explore and have adventure? (Please note these needs are not gender specific.)

Your inner child is a sub personality of you and a very real factor of our present day experience. Your identity, self beliefs and your unconscious behaviours, all stem from experience as a child. If your child was not happy or unfulfilled, as a child, then your adult experience is a perfect stage in life for the child to safely express. Your child knows this intuitively. Your inner child wants you to be happy and wants to give you experiences that heal the past.

Undeveloped parts of your personality and identity will be triggered as you step forward into new challenges and changes of life as an adult.

Your inner child's underdeveloped growth will trigger adulthood circumstances and experience that the inner child will deem necessary for the integrated growth and development of the whole person.

Find him or her, cuddle them and love you through them, everyday. In time your true inner self will start to emerge. The precious child in you wants expression, love and acknowledgment that it did not receive as a child.

34
YOUR FAMILY BOND

When you were growing up in your family, you learnt about emotions and who you were through the mirror of your primary caregivers, your parents. This experience of life becomes an emotionally bonding relationship, whether healthy, toxic or neutral. Trust is fostered by the fact that you come to expect and rely on the responses of your caregivers. This response became your mirror of who you are. The bond became the interpersonal bridge between child and caregiver and is the mutual foundation for your growth and understanding of the world. What travelled along this bridge, between you and your primary caregivers, becomes the understanding of your world and what you see in the mirror. It becomes your identity. If your caregivers were suppressed emotionally and unloving towards themselves, that is reflected in the mirror and you have taken this mirroring on as an identity.

Parents who are shut down emotionally cannot mirror or acknowledge a child's emotions. They cannot affirm something that they do not feel, first within themselves. Loss of mirroring has the effect of abandonment to a child. Without someone to mirror you have no way of knowing who you really are. A false sense of self becomes your identity. There is no blame here, only acknowledgment of your inner child's needs not being able to be fully expressed and nurtured, as a child. Loving you today, is imperative to reclaiming your true authentic self, as you peel back the false self.

The false self is littered with negative emotions and responses that limit you from your full loving potential. It is hard to love ourselves deeper when there is guilt and shame, layered over your true self.

Shame and guilt are two of the most destructive emotions that we have been mirrored and that we suppress. Loving oneself was deemed in earlier generations as wrong and guilt was attached. Guilt learnt as a child covers a deeper internalised energy that is the feeling of shame. This feeling of shame, leads us to cover up our true self, we act in a shameless manner (as if we have no shame and judge and project it onto others, passive aggressive, controlling, criticising, rigid) or we act out shamefully. (Out of control, failure, gluttonous, obsessive and compulsive.)

Your ongoing self love journey will uncover deeper and deeper layers of shame and guilt, please love yourself even more in awareness as these feelings surface. Accept with love and compassion all parts of you and all your feelings, as you journey back to spiritual and emotional healing.

I recommend facilitation by conscious healers and therapists, to support your grief work to heal your inner child. I have been blessed to watch the transformation of many beautiful souls through their commitment and love to their child as they participate and shine through the delivery of the Inner Child Workshops. Understanding and recovery from your grief, guilt & shame, low self esteem, addictions and compulsions, frees you to live a more authentic life. John Bradshaw is one of the most world leading experts in healing shame and the interpersonal dynamics of family systems, I recommend reading his classics 'Healing the Shame that Binds You' and 'The Family'.

35
SENSUALITY

Everything around us is energy and if you open up to it, you can experience sensuality in all that you touch and share. Nature and the air you breathe allows for the experience of sensuality to flow.

Sensuality is a deep experience of divine love and it is accessible to you every moment. The experience of your own inner sensuality leads to increased awareness and sensitivity to your surroundings. You tune in. Sensuality highlights universal oneness and who you are at your core essence.

Opening yourself to an expanded feeling of sensuality is to experience self love.

When you experience JOY as feeling, tasting, smelling, touching you participate in the delight of your connectedness to all things. This is the 'feeling' of sensuality although words are limited. It is really an experience to be felt.

36
SENSUALITY MEDITATION

Find a safe place alone to practice this meditation.

Maybe your bedroom or another room that is private, where no one will enter.

Fit yourself into as little clothing as possible to allow yourself to feel your own body easily.

Lie down on your bed. Relax your arms out to the side. Open up your palms, relaxing the fingers. Relax your legs and let yourself melt into the bed, allow yourself to feel all your body from your feet to your fingers as your body opens up and relaxes.

Become aware of the air around you and how it feels on your skin and how it is coming in and out of your body. Breathe in and allow the breath to spread itself around all the parts of your body that may be tight or holding on, just allow the breath to find its own rhythm.

If your mind is filled with chatter and thoughts about the day or about this process, release them and let them go.

Feel your body sink your awareness into your stomach and thighs. Surrender to the air around you. Allow the air to penetrate all parts of your body that you notice; your fingers, your shoulders, your throat. Feel the warmth.

Imagine the day or night is touching you, as the air is, feel the cycles of the seasons and cycles of your body and how intertwined they are. Allow your heart to open and expand. Your heart's love filters through your body and meets the air. Continue to breathe and relax, melting into your surroundings as if everything is one.

Allow yourself to fully feel the light around you as love. Let light touch you. You are love. You are loved. Touch with your fingertips the air around you and touch gently your body, with the presence of love through your hands. Sense any colours around you. Feel the Joy of YOU in this safe warm space.

Do this process as often as you can and expand the experience by going without clothes. Be naked; release yourself from the metaphorical layers of hurt and shyness by removing the clothing. Be authentic. Let love in. Surrender to your own love.

The more often you do it, the deeper you will go.

Take yourself a step further and willingly allow your fantasy lover to enter the room, letting him or her get as close as you can tolerate. Lucid dreaming is vital to exploring you.

37
LOVE

Love is

Love mediates healings

Love creates

Love is transformational

Love created your body and the earth love can recreate it

Love allows light to shine and come forth as information

Loves shines light on darkness and fear and it dissipates

Love softens our mind and ego

We are love – finding your way back is the self love journey

38
LOVING PROCESSES

Life is a process. Love is a process. To love yourself, utilise processes. Release built up energy that is the opposite to love. Observe your thoughts, beliefs, actions and process them into empowerment and a positive charge.

Scientists tell us that when we simply observe ourselves, we affect the sub atomic field. This means change does happen. Daily processes do have a powerful, loving effect.

Mindfulness

Do you ever find yourself wondering where the day went? Have you found that you feel detached from what you are doing? Are you trying yet not content or happy? Are you struggling to make sense of what you do?

If so, bring your full attention to what you are doing.

The process of mindfulness means is to master your attention into the present.

Bring your attention to the present when sitting or in outcome focussed events such as cooking, driving, working or attending to errands.

Turn off distractions and allow your attention to be on one thing at a time.

Practice periods of silence and stillness helps to develop your mind to unclog the clutter of unwanted thoughts and emotions. This is the beginning of meditation.

Bring your attention fully to whatever it is that you are doing. A connection to source love and self will renew itself.

Mindfulness is a way of reducing your stress and allowing the body to be fully immersed in the now. Whether you are on the freeway or in nature, really bring your attention to what you are doing and how you are doing it.

It is not 'what' you are doing that is important; it is in the 'how' you are doing it that is more important.

Give your fullest attention, to whatever the moment presents. Life force begins to flow through you into whatever you are engaged in.

The more mindful you are, the more relaxed you are. The body-mind will sync together, resulting in better decision making, reduced stress and most importantly being present with you and with those you love.

Fear

Has fear stopped you? Fear is disempowering, yet there is always an opportunity to choose more love within a fear based emotion. There is always somewhere better for you to reach for, if you look at the negative situation or challenge as an opportunity to expand into more love for you.

Fear brings on denial, confusions and conflict and is reflected in these limiting beliefs and thoughts:

- I'm not good enough.
- I can't do that.
- I'm not deserving or worthy.
- I want that but I don't believe I will get it.

Love is of a light/high vibration, fear is a dark/low vibration.

If you feel fear, use it as another opportunity to choose love.

Everything is energy, thoughts are energy, feelings are energy.

Fear is an energy that can be changed into something else.

Fear can propel you forward. It can be a motivating force and when it does move you to action the fear has turned into a resource. The action is coming from a lower vibration than love but it is working for you. Love that!

Let compassion flow to the fear. Love the fear as if it was a stubborn child.

When you observe 'fear' just observe it and let yourself feel into it quietly detached. Let the fear be felt and release itself.

You are an infinite being with choice and free will here. You have choice to feel love over fear.

The Gift of Forgiveness for You

Hurt resentment and grievances are energy. It is a negative energy that creates more negative emotions and experiences. Letting go and forgiving from your heart will change your internal state even at stressful times. Forgiveness is a *gift* to you and them.

Read through this section fully first, then come back to here and start the process….

Forgiveness from the Heart:

- ♥ Let your heart feel a memory of love from the past, present or future (like that of the unconditional love from a child or family member).

- ♥ Allow the warmth and buzz of love to move through your body and out through your aura.

- ♥ Imagine your can open up your Heart, to feel the love more

- ♥ Now that your Heart Chakra is open…bring a small version of yourself (like a shrink doll) into your Heart's energy….and feel the love and acceptance.

- ♥ Let your symbolic arms reach around you (the little version) and HUG you. Really HUG.

- ♥ Melt into this….and exhale fully, to let go of what you have been consciously or unconsciously hanging onto.

- ♥ Now effortlessly forgive yourself, your sub-personalities, your mind, your sabotages, all the parts of you, all the shoulds', the guilt, all the emotions you feel. Let it all go, let yourself be loved by you a little deeper.

- ♥ Can you now shrink the other person in your life (who is teaching you something about yourself) and forgive them. Just forgive them for all that they do or don't do that hurts you or offends you.

- ♥ Look for the teaching and meaning that they bring to your life and spirit. There is always meaning and insight. What is the opportunity to grow into love? Even the most perceived negative situation has an insight for you.

- ♥ Let the love flow out of your heart and out to them. Release them from the negative connection they have with you. A new dawn is coming and the energy is changing.

- ♥ Let yourself move through deeper and deeper levels of love now. Love for yourself, for your heart, spirit and soul.

- ♥ Breathe, breathe, breathe.

Treat yourself like your own best friend

New Dawn Meditation

- ♥ Imagine you are on the edge of the world there is the hint of the early morning around you, just before the sun is ready to rise.

- ♥ See yourself clearly.

- ♥ Stand with two feet, hip width apart.

- ♥ Feel the anticipation of more, light coming into your world, into your energy field and into your body.

- ♥ As the sun gets closer to rising you take a breath in and you take in more light.

- ♥ The breath and sunlight find a feeling, a part of you that doesn't feel light, observe what that is without attachment.

- ♥ Now release that feeling or darkness with an exhalation and as you exhale, let it go…. notice the sensation as it leaves your body.

- ♥ Observe how any new spaces are being filled with love and light as the day grows lighter. There is more, light around and within you.

Repeat

Heart Felt Clarity Meditation
A process for feeling your core heart desires.

Read through the process first, and then come back to this point. Take your time.

Let yourself feel it. The more you feel, the more you will release the formations of layers or emotions and conditioning about *'how you should feel'* or what you have *'suppressed'*.

Some feelings will be raw and intense and it will feel like you are digging through rock. The more you can feel it without attaching and stopping the feelings the clearer in your heart answers will appear. After time this process allows you to feel your heart and clear the channel for more love.

It is my experience that when you can reach core clarity of the heart, circumstances change instantly around you. The ability to be in your heart gives you a clarity that will always guide you on your true path. Decisions are easier and realities change in an instant.

If you cannot feel anything at first, keep your attention on what you see and keep breathing. Suppressed feelings are good at hiding, it will take patience and love for them to appear and be felt.

My suggestion is to do this process every third day, to start with. Then after two weeks, use this skill when you feel confused or stressed. Write down in a journal after you have finished what feelings you observed. It is very interesting for your mind to observe this process afterwards and not during.

If you do slip into your logic, then move back down into your heart and feel again.

Heart Felt Clarity

There are layers of your heart that are like the shale layers of rock and sediment. Just like rock formations over time, this layering of your heart has built up over time and forms the layering of our conditioning.

- ♥ If you could see the first layer; what would it look like?
- ♥ Does it look like hard rock? Or is it more like shale?
- ♥ If you could feel the first layer; what does it feel like?
- ♥ Let the feeling wash over you
- ♥ Observe how the layer falls away and dissipates
- ♥ As the next layer comes into focus; feel it or see it.
- ♥ If you see it; look for feeling you can see and recognise
- ♥ Then move down through the layer and watch the layer disappear…..feel through the next deeper layer of shale
- ♥ What do you feel?
- ♥ What do you see? As you look and feel just breathe in and out, aware of letting go of the sensation within

- ♥ If you feel like crying, let it happen, let the feeling wash over you

- ♥ As you recognise or feel the meaning of the layer, the layer will dissipate and you can go deeper…….down through the layers.

- ♥ Keep moving through the layers, feeling as you go and getting closer to your core heart's desire.

- ♥ Some layers will be joyful, loving and freeing; others will be anger, frustration, self hate etc.

- ♥ There is no right or wrong emotion and no order to be followed with the flow of your feelings.

- ♥ Keep going until you feel and find your pure heart's desire.

- ♥ You will know when, you have got to the core of what you want. It will be clarity. It may be an insight as to how you want to feel. It will feel like you have hit the jackpot.

- ♥ For each of us it will be different feeling, value or sense of direction.

- ♥ With this heart insight, you will be able to move forward in love….and the whole world will move aside for you, all perceived limits will collapse. As you move forward in love all will be perfect in your world and shoulds' and should nots will have no more shame and power over your heart.

- ♥ Feel your heart's desire and let it be your guiding light. Your core heart's desire will feel like you have found gold.

The Mirror

This caring mirror process works with your unconscious and conscious mind.

Everyday stand in front of the mirror looking at yourself and say one of the loving statements below until you start and continue to receive acceptance feelings and thoughts.

For instance look at the mirror and look directly into your own eyes and say "I Love You" over and over again. Listen deeply and pay attention to the signs and reactions of your body and feelings.

You may find yourself squirm, wiggle and want to look away as feelings of *self hate* surface as guilt and shame.

Do not give up! This exercise is working at profound shifts in your unconscious. It will feel like you are drilling and it will be confronting. What you are seeking is space for love and to remove impediments to feeling your own love. Keep persisting with this process even if it feels futile. Feelings of self-distrust and self-hate have been buried within your heart and cells over this lifetime and from other previous lives and these feelings need to be cracked and released with loving presence and compassion.

The deep pressure of guilt and shame needs to be released and felt, so that you feel that you are indeed, lovable.

Use these statements daily in front of the mirror:

- ♥ I love you
- ♥ I approve of you
- ♥ I accept you
- ♥ I deserve to have……..
- ♥ I love myself
- ♥ I am Beautiful

The additional process is to look at a part of your body in the mirror that you have not yet accepted as lovable and beautiful. Look to the area of your body i.e.: nose, breasts, thighs and say; "I love you" or "You are beautiful", over and over until you come into loving acceptance for that part of you. Over time what you once did not like or love about yourself can become vibrating with love and gentleness so much so that everyone else will then affirm as you and your body as beautiful also. Sounds like magic…it is and you are magical. You can love you!

Affirmations

Affirmations harmonise your mental energy with your heart energy and give you a powerful focus.

- ♥ I am energy and my story is energy and can be remoulded and reshaped with love and compassion.
- ♥ Love is the only path to Divine Power. I am love. I am Divine Power.
- ♥ I love myself and accept myself unconditionally.
- ♥ I love myself as I am.
- ♥ I am loving and I am loveable.
- ♥ I can choose my thoughts.
- ♥ I do what I love and love what I do.
- ♥ The more I love what I do, the more I can do what I love.
- ♥ When I am inspired by love, there are infinite possibilities.
- ♥ I graciously love all the relationships in my life, as they allow me to see and feel the real me, so I learn to love myself more.
- ♥ I surrender the suffering; I am enough.

- ♥ On every first waking moment, say with open heart and warmth: "I Love You *insert your name*". As if a lover or loving parent was greeting you.

- ♥ I am the author of my own love story.

- ♥ I choose to feel….

- ♥ I choose to believe that I can.

- ♥ I am all knowing, all healing and all powerful.

- ♥ Everything is in perfect balance for the loving conscious expansion of my heart and soul.

- ♥ Challenges and blocks are opportunities to feel the healing power of unconditional love for myself and others.

- ♥ The more resentment I release the more space I will have to feel love.

- ♥ I open my heart to feel the love of this present moment.

- ♥ I am healed as I open my heart.

- ♥ I listen with love to my body's messages.

- ♥ I listen to my emotions as signposts and respond lovingly.

- ♥ I choose to believe that my desires will manifest for the highest good, in love and light.

- ♥ I am grateful for my fears as they allow me to choose more love.
- ♥ I know that illness and stress are messages from my heart and soul and I am grateful for this wisdom.
- ♥ Even if I don't see the perfection of life in this moment, I know there is balance.
- ♥ I trust in the process of life.
- ♥ I am willing to release the need of not loving myself.
- ♥ I am willing to change.
- ♥ I deserve the best and accept it now.
- ♥ I love myself therefore it is ok to feel good.
- ♥ The choice is mine.
- ♥ All is well.
- ♥ I am a vibrant, joyful being of light and love; every cell in my body radiates love, health and joy.

Decision Making

Assertive, present decision making is self love.

Have your options ready at hand, to assess the best choice.

- ♥ Pause and become very present within your body.
- ♥ Become aware of your body without judgement.
- ♥ Which parts of your body are tense? Release the tension.
- ♥ How is your sense of balance? Adjust your left and right to gain balance.
- ♥ Feel into the connection between all parts of your body.
- ♥ Which parts feel at ease and which parts feel uncomfortable.
- ♥ Visualise the body lovingly connecting as one harmonious vessel.
- ♥ Ask yourself; what do I want? How do I want to feel?
- ♥ Am I resourced to make this decision? Do I need more information to feel resourced? If so lovingly give yourself more space and time to gather information. E.g. Make calls complete research etc to get comfortable.
- ♥ Once you know how you want to feel, allow that feeling to start growing either by visualisation or

remembering a memory of past when you have felt this way before.

♥ Now you are aligned to the feeling, which option resonates with you the most?

♥ What decision feels right now? Trust the impulse and go with that decision. Make a choice. Commit with full intention that you are on your path in love.

♥ With gratitude, thank yourself and move forward into action immediately or make a plan to implement your decision. Smile into your heart and congratulate yourself.

Smiling into your heart, 'I am enough'

A Meditative Process to Feel Your Heart

- ♥ Gently breathe in through the nose and out through the mouth. Inhale and exhale very slowly and long... feel your core...allow the breath to find its way...let the focus of the mind be on the breath, gently quieten all the brain noise and sub-personalities who want to have a say.

- ♥ Feel your heart within your body, feel its warmth and energy.

- ♥ Visualise your heart with the edges softening.

- ♥ Rub your heart region with your hands to get the vibration following through your body.

- ♥ Breathe in love, breathe out confusion and fear. Repeat a couple of times, feeling more love flowing and filling your body.

- ♥ Silently or out loud ask your heart a question about a challenge, your direction, and a lesson or ask for a direct clear decision from a question that gives a yes or no answer.

- ♥ Listen carefully and wait for an answer. It may come as an impulse, a picture, a symbol, a word, it also may feel like a nudge, feeling or insight.

♥ Whatever the answer, it will come with a feeling of *'knowing'* that feels warm and positive. It is a high vibration of love.

Intentions

After opening and feeling your heart in the above meditation it is a perfect time to set a Heart Intention while your heart's energy is clear:

- ♥ With the answer, from your the Heart, claim your intention.

- ♥ Feeling the energy from the heart, what action you will take?

- ♥ Engage your heart and mind to make a conscious decision about what action you will take?

Claiming your intention (like setting a goal) with your heart is so much more powerful than with the mind alone. When you set the Intention with the heart, your whole body and energy field adjusts to a new alignment. The result is, you are clear and you will move towards your intention more easily and the mind aligns with the heart.

Your reality works on intention.

Heartfelt intentions create your reality...

The Balancing Effect of Intention Energy:

Once you set an intention: sometimes you will observe the balancing effect.

Intention setting from the heart is one chord of the equation, a major chord to catch your future wave of potential. The next chord is to prepare for the anti-intentions and to compassionately feel the fear.

Preparing by writing down all the challenges and negativities that you may experience as you move towards your intention is useful to your mind and shadow personalities. What are the balancing effects you can expect? What on-track signs will there be?

- ♥ What are your balancing fears? What fears are yet to be faced?
- ♥ How will life change for you as you move towards your goal?
- ♥ What skills do you have to learn, to be the person you need to be to in order to allow your intention to manifest?
- ♥ What will you *let go* of to reach your goal?
- ♥ What challenges will be proof that you are creating the life you have asked for?
- ♥ How will you self love through this process?

While moving towards intentions you have to act, feel and think as a person who already has achieved the intention. This could mean a stage of chaos as limiting beliefs collapse. Maximum growth happens on the cusp of chaos and order. Enjoy this stage.

In writing down the anti-intentions your mind and heart get a clear picture of what your life will look and feel as you move towards your intention. You can relax, you are prepared.

Grounding

Grounding is a feeling of connectedness. Other ways of describing this feeling is; being centred, relaxed, in your body, embodiment.

You ground your body by connecting to the ground. Mother earth will help you stabilise and create an anchor of peace within. We are connected to all systems, matrixes and energy grids and the most important grid is the connection to the ground.

The Earth element is what brings all the yet to be manifested into manifestation in this physical reality.

This process can be done whenever you feel heady, overwhelmed, stressed or off centre.

Connect yourself to the ground. Feel the ground through your feet. Become aware of the ground and how it supports you.

A good process is while you are standing, with your feet hip width apart, exhaling gently bend your knees just slightly, tilt your hips forward and imagine a fishing line is running from your Base Chakra to the ground. (Base Chakra lies in the area of the coccyx for men and between the ovaries for women)

Feel the support in your body.

Send any excess energy to the ground through your feet.

Feel the ground as you make choices about what you want to experience.

Feel the stability and harmony of being aligned to create your reality here on this earth.

Remember the metaphor of the Vine…it grows and reaches as it spreads while it is firmly rooted within the ground.

Soften your Heart

Close your eyes and relax your shoulders, take in three deep breaths, releasing the breath slowly as you exhale.

Visualise your heart within your body, looking at it literally and feeling it.

What does it feel like?

What does it look like?

If the edges are sharp and harsh, just soften the edges.

Release through your breath all harshness...

Use a soft brush as a helpful tool to soften the edges of your heart.

Watch your heart melting and the edges softening..

What colour does your heart radiate? What colour would you like it to be more of; red, pink...or maybe green....allow more of that colour to glow out of your heart..

Feel your heart responding by the resulting sensation of relaxation.

Emotional Freedom Technique

This technique is one of the most empowering self help processes, it instantly changes your internal state to feeling relief.

EFT, as we refer to it, is meridian tapping, a healing tool based on the body's subtle energy systems and meridians, to relieve and release the emotional blocks in the body, releasing the trapped emotions, you don't have to know where it is trapped. Emotions are 'energy in motion'. Tapping all the points of the energetic body, releases the emotions where they are stuck, without having to know where the glitch has happened.

You start by repeating this affirmation:

"Even though I feel '………………..', I deeply and completely accept and love myself".

You allow acceptance and love, to flow to whatever is to be loved and accepted about you. EFT can give you clarity as to 'why' you feel the way you do. It will help you *feel* better.

EFT is a powerful technique at also lessening pain and treating unwanted symptoms of illness and disease. The internet is full of information about this valuable self help technique. Go to www.balancedbeing.com.au to download EFT PDF instructions.

39
I LOVE MYSELF

The universe loves me. Deep within me is a well of unending love. A source endless and full. I am beloved by the source. My behaviours and thoughts reflect the inner expression of this magnificent love. I feel love vibrate through everything I touch and put my attention on. I love myself. I love myself deeper as I learn how to. I am therefore a radiant blessing in this body. I am love blossoming. Everything I need to know about myself is revealed to me in perfect timing. I am perfectly poised to emerge into my own self loving evolution. I am an infinite being that knows boundless love and joy and my daily play is to reveal more of that day after day. I love myself, therefore I enjoy myself. I love myself therefore all that I am is vibrationally aligned with what surrounds me; lifting friendships, wonderful family relationships, a healthy body and mind and a perfect combination of expressed purpose and balance as I choose to create abundance and success through my chosen career path.. There is infinite wisdom available to me, it comes forth and it feels good. Wisdom and knowledge fills my being, my heart, my body and my mind. Every action I take is an expression of this love and I allow more. I share love freely with others and love expands throughout humanity and is multiplied. I lay open to receive more love in grace and humility.

I love therefore I am.

40
LOVE IS UNENDING IN POTENTIAL

These words are a gift of love, open up your heart to receive them. Words are my love language. When I write it is an expression of love. When you receive them with full heart, you feel the love and the love expands. The truth is I love you. When you allow me expression, I love more of myself. When you love yourself, I will witness that love and feel more love. Heartfelt thanks for sharing in this feast of love.

Self love is to honour, respect, forgive, accept and love yourself. In loving yourself you have the ability to change internal and external environments; that is, our relationships with our partner, children, finances, career, business structures, family dynamics and long held conditioning. The world environment changes, nature responds lovingly, local communities shift as our being shifts. Most importantly the temple of your body becomes the embodiment of love. You are both healer and consciousness as one.

Your internal harmony will reflect to the outer world. As you heal, with love so will the environment and mother earth. You are a spiritual being having a physical experience and as spirit you are connected to every living system on the planet and into the universe. It is up to us to transcend the old patterns and conditions of love to let in the new fuller lover energies that will emerge through us as full soul consciousness arrives on the planet. Love will be the only energy and our bodies will anchor that love. Through self love you can align and open up your heart ready to receive love's clarity.

Gracefully yours in love and light

Allanah

More information on Allanah at www.balancedbeing.com.au

www.ingramcontent.com/pod-product-compliance
Lightning Source LLC
Chambersburg PA
CBHW051804040426
42446CB00007B/510